How to Get a Job

Perfect Answers to Difficult Interview Questions and Tips on How to Succeed in Interviews

By

Garry Bolton

Table of Contents

Introduction

To be honest, a pending job interview can be very daunting. You will definitely want to succeed in an interview, and you would love to be remembered after you leave. This book will give you all the information you need, as it is full of useful interview tips and applicable examples.

Research suggests that you have only five minutes to make a favorable impression and that some interviewers have decided within the first thirty seconds whether or not they like you as a person. With these statistics in mind, you are encouraged to *read* and use the interview tips provided in this book to ensure your success in the interview.

In Chapter 1, you are guided through the various types of interviews that you should expect, and the process each takes has been outlined.

In Chapter 2, you are prepared for the interview so that you feel positive enough to carry it off confidently.

In Chapter 3, some advice is provided regarding the best ways to present yourself with a maximum effect in getting a job.

In Chapter 4, those *difficult interview questions* are addressed. We look at ten tricky questions and give you an idea on how best to answer them. Also, you are provided with some guide on answering 'inappropriate' interview questions. Furthermore, we shall also look at five *behaviour-based interview questions* and provide you with thoughts of how best to respond to them.

In Chapter 5, we will consider *statements* that should be avoided in an interview and why.

In Chapter 6, you will be guided through the last stage of the interview, and you will be shown how to finish strong.

By means of this book, you will understand your strength, through your actions, in such a purposeful way that will make any potential employer find you appealing.

Chapter 1 - What is a Job Interview and Why is It Necessary?

Starting with a simple definition of a job interview, a job interview is a business meeting in which an interviewee is asked questions to determine their suitability for a specific job at a particular company. An interview needs to take place for both the company and the applicant to get to know each other better so that they can decide whether or not to pursue the relationship. In a way, it is like a first date.

Different Types of Interviews

Let us briefly consider the different types of interviews you may encounter.

On-line interviews: These most frequently take place in real-time with a webcam. They are a simple, cost-effective method of interviewing, especially during the early stages of recruitment. It is convenient because no one has to travel, especially if the position for which you are applying is in a different city.

Online interviews carry as much weight as face-to-face interviews, so be sure to dress correctly; remove clutters from the area that will appear on camera, choose a quiet room where you will not be interrupted, have a pen and paper ready to make notes, and have a copy of your CV close for referral purposes (just in case your nerves make you forgetful).

Telephone interviews: As with all interactions involving a prospective employer, you should take a telephone interview seriously. At this stage, the hiring company is probably calling a dozen or more candidates in order to narrow the field and decide who gets invited to the next round of the interview. If you are too lax in your preparation and do not take the telephone interview seriously, it may be the last call you get from the company.

Face-to-face interviews: These are the more customary types of interviews, and they may take various forms. You may be interviewed by one person or by a panel. You may be alone or part of a group. There are two keys to succeed in this type of interview situation; *listen* well and know *when* to speak. Do not speak purely for the sake of having something to say. If you need a moment to think before you answer a difficult question, feel free to ask for a minute to gather your thoughts, rather than rambling off on a tangent while hoping your brain catches up with your tongue sooner.

Pay attention to what those around you are asking and saying; reiterate things that you have heard to show that you have been listening. For example, in a group interview you may say something like, 'I agree with Mike, training is important. I believe that if staff members are trained properly, they work more efficiently. However, to prevent unnecessary expense to the company, training should not be compulsory. It should be an option for those who wish to grow in their fields.

Behavior-centered interviews: This type of interviews situation is becoming more popular. These consultations comprise of questions pertaining to how you handled past situations, as opposed to the more traditional interview that covers your qualifications and work experience. The reasoning behind *behaviour-based* interviews is that past behavior forecasts future performance. In this type of interview, you understand your strengths and weaknesses as well as your talents and abilities, and then couple them with real life situations that can serve as examples which illustrate your skills.

For you to be relaxed, you can contact the interviewing company ahead of time to enquire the form the interview takes. This will provide you with enough time to prepare and practice for your interview. We will cover this topic in detail in Chapter 2.

Chapter 2 - The Perfect Interview is the One You are Well Prepared for

Applying the three "R's" to your interview preparation

Research + Rehearse + Result

Research the Job

Most ads will mention responsibilities that go with the position you are applying for as well as the qualities that the company is looking for in its employees. Paying attention to these requirements will help you ensure that the job is a good fit for you.

By using the information in the advertisement, you can promote your specific skills and capabilities. You can then work these accomplishments into your interview preparation.

Gearing up for a behaviour-based interview

Your preparation for this type of interview is slightly more personal. Questions are tailored to determine *how* you have responded to different situations in the past in order to gauge whether you will fit in with the company in future. You cannot arrive at a behaviour-based interview without having taken the time to do some groundwork. You need to be able to describe your experiences as clearly as possible, focusing on your strengths and abilities, and highlighting your successes.

To achieve this, you start by making a list of the job requirements (this information is available in the advert or on the company website). Next, make a list of your skills

that closely match the requirements and then write down instances where you applied the skills. For example: The position calls for an engineer who has a sustainable approach to environmental issues. In your previous job, you were tasked with finding sustainable ways in which hot water could be made available in poor rural areas. You introduced solar heating systems to the communities and provided workshops to teach them how to look after the equipment so that your company's maintenance overheads were reduced. Your practical experience proves that you not only have the qualification, you also have the expertise. An easy formula to help you remember this principle is: Job requirement + Your skill + Real life situation = Question answered effectively.

Research the Firm

You need to prove that you are interested enough in the job and the company and that you've done some research on them before you arrived for the interview. The most effective place to find the information that you need

is the company's own website. Use your research to answer these questions:

What does the company look for in their candidates?

Knowing what the establishment looks for in their candidates will enable you to position yourself as the ideal applicant.

Who are the key people in the organization?

Get to know the names of those who hold significant positions in the company. One or more of them may even be present at your interview.

What is the latest news on the company?

Familiarize yourself with current news so that if the opportunity arises, you are able to converse on the subject during the interview.

Explore the company's culture, mission, and values?

Statistics show that 43% of hiring authorities believe that cultural fit is the most important quality to look for whilst interviewing candidates. You can discover more about this side of the corporation on their social media pages. For example, you are invited to attend an interview for the position of graphic designer at The Big Heart Company. Upon doing some research on their website and

the Facebook page, you discover that they are a faith-based organization, actively involved in mission work and community service. If your goal is to climb the corporate ladder and make a name for yourself in the design field, you may want to reconsider your suitability for *this* position.

Who are the company's clients?

Knowing the names of some of the company's clients may allow you an opportunity to drop some all-important names during your interview. This will also prove to your interviewer that you did some finding.

Research the Interviewing Panel

It would benefit you greatly to know the name of the CEO or MD of the company as well as those of the directors or managers. This information is available on the company's 'About Us' page and under employer's biographies. If you know the name of the person who will be interviewing you, you can do a bit of research on LinkedIn or Twitter. You are looking for their employment history, their achievements, or a little piece of common ground. You might discover that you went to the same college with one of the directors, or that you both enjoy hiking. You just need a little morsel to add significance to your interview, if the opportunity comes. You should know that the interviewer has done a bit of research on your profile, return the favor so that you are equally matched.

Rehearse

You have heard the expression "practice makes perfect," well this is true for your interview too. Preparing what you want to say *in your head* is not the same as speaking it out loud. The way you speak to your friends and family every day is not quite the same as in an interview situation. Practice the industry's phraseology, especially if the position you are applying for is in a different field. Practice in front of the mirror, practice with a friend or family member or record yourself speaking and listen to yourself with a critical ear. Make notes of the feedback you get (from yourself and others) and work on

honing your elocution skills. By practicing the answers to difficult or tricky questions repeatedly, you will find it easier and more natural to answer them in a nerve-wracking interview situation.

Another thing you should practice often before your interview is speaking about your selling points. What are your strengths? What are you great at? What have you accomplished that sets you apart? What do you have that will add value to this company? Often, we are too modest, and therefore we do not sell ourselves. Modesty will mask your accomplishments. Loudly and confidently proclaim what you are capable of while you drive to work, when you're in the shower, and as you prepare dinner. You can even tell your pet. The more you proclaim it and the more you hear it, the more confident you will feel sharing this all-important information with your interviewer.

Results

There is no secret recipe or shortcut – hard work leads to desired results. If you implement the principles set out in this book, you can be rest assured that you will be ready for anything your interviewers have up their sleeves.

Chapter 3 - Sell Yourself

Introduce yourself to your interviewer with a smile and a firm handshake and maintain polite eye contact throughout the interview. Knowing *when* to speak and when to *stop* speaking in an interview is as important as knowing what to say. Your interviewer wants to know about you, and what you have to offer the company, so you will be given opportunities to sell yourself. You need to recognize and respond to these openings.

Certain questions are *entry points* that give you the chance to elaborate on your capabilities. A question like,

Can you tell me something about yourself?' doesn't give you the time to mention the size of your family or the number of pets you own. No, this is the time to say that you are a hard working individual who pays attention to details, or that you are a natural leader and problem-solver. Be assertive even if you don't feel confident. Avoid complaining or negative comments. Reiterate your interest in the company and the job which you are applying for.

Appear Decent

Decide on what to wear before the day of the interview and have a backup plan in case of laundry or wardrobe malfunction. Check if the suit you wore to your last interview, five years ago, doesn't fit that well anymore – you have to change it. Dress for success. This goes without saying, but some people neglect this. One way you can gauge the best way to dress for an interview is to observe how the employees of the company dress and then raise it a notch. If you are unable to find this information by visiting the company or the company's website, then it is safest to dress smart and appear a little conservative. Your clothes should look smart so that you leave a semantic hook associated with you in the interviewer's memory. For a successful interview, the semantic hook should be positive. Such an accessory of a man as a bright-colored tie of the "eating-out" eye, rather, will cause irritation. A lady should not wear expensive jewelry to an interview. You can limit yourself to elegant jewelry. It should be beautiful and elegant, add confidence and attract the attention of the interlocutor. Rather avoid expensive perfume or cologne and stick with a tried and trusted antiperspirant. Often, interviews are scheduled one after another and the mix of perfumes and colognes in the interview room may become quite overpowering for the interviewer. People cause sympathy because they look nice and interesting. And what they say is better remembered. For you, this is what you need.

Body language is important. Sitting with your arms crossed tightly throughout the interview is not going to count well in your favor. Don't slouch or stare at the floor. Maintain eye contact with the interviewer. Look into the interviewer's eyes (or at least in the direction of the interlocutor). Almost all people are able to interpret the feelings of the interlocutor on the movements of the eyes at a subconscious level. Lean forward in your chair slightly to show that you are interested in what your interviewer has to say. If you are being interviewed in a group, look at the person who is talking and nod your head if you are in agreement. On the flipside, do not shake your head if you disagree – an interview is not the place to start a debate or show signs of negativity.

Most people gesticulate while talking. Do not deny yourself this. Do not try to appear perfect. Non-aggressive gesticulation has to you a companion because it often helps to speak better and more clearly. Try not to invent and don't lie – most recruiters will immediately notice if you do because they are constantly working with job seekers. Don't say inappropriate statements or phrases. Do not let this happen even if the interview is over and you just talk to the recruiter. Remember that you are constantly assessed.

Things to Take in and Leave out

The following tips are needed for a successful interview.

Carry a small card with keywords to help prompt you during a blank moment. Have a pen close at hand in case you want to make a note of something or remind yourself of a question you have the opportunity to ask later in the interview.

Having a copy of your CV close to you in case you need to refer to dates or the order of past employments (interview nerves can cause you to forget the simplest of things); you may also want to offer a copy of your CV to the interviewer in case they don't have one with them.

Arrive for the interview about fifteen minutes before time, to allow yourself time to unwind from your commute. Take some time to read through your CV to recharge your brain and psych yourself up for the interview.

Don't chew gum during your interview and don't walk in carrying a cup of coffee.

Leave your cell phone and other electronic devices in the car, or if you must have them with you, make sure they are switched off or in silence.

Gaps in Your Employment

Don't ignore gaps in your employment history in the hopes that no one will notice. Rather address them promptly and positively to avoid any misunderstandings. Whether the gap was forced or voluntary, be open and honest when invited to discuss it. Mention ventures that you were involved in during the time you were unemployed; things like child rearing, further studies, freelance work, consulting work, caring for a sick relative, volunteer work or community projects will help you effectively fill in the gaps. If you were retrenched, talk about the company restructuring which led to your redundancy. This is a common occurrence and needn't be shied away from. If you were dismissed be ready to explain the situation. Above all, be honest.

Stress and Experience are Two Companions of the Competitor

Are you worried that you can't make an adequate decision? Find the right formulations to adequately present yourself. Before you go into the interviewer's office, devote a few minutes for yourself. Shake your hands, break your fingers and move the jaws in different directions for a minute or two. If there are no video cameras in the waiting room or in the hall where you are, you can even wave your hands. Breathe as if you are doing some yoga. Breathe deeply and in a measured manner, counting up to four between inspiration and exhalation. This activates the speech centers, soothes the brain and relieves nervous tension.

Take a notebook and make notes in it during the conversation. This will give you time to think through the questions and present yourself as a trained person. Write the same advice there. Straighten your back, smile, do not jerk your foot and be thankful for the meeting; remember this interview will not cause a crash of the planet or your life. Nothing will change – in fact, you will forget about everything in a day. It is possible that the interviewer will forget you at the receipt of the next applicant. Just talk with the benefit for yourself; ask yourself questions about the company, the team, the corporate culture, etc. Use the principle of win-win – even if you do not get this job, you will have some experience. This can be used for its further development.

Chapter 4 - Difficult Interview Questions and How Best to Answer Them

Questions type 1: Can you tell me about yourself?

The trick to answering this question correctly is to strike a balance between your personal life and your career. Answering this question, the most important thing is to explain to the employer how you can be useful to the company in the position you are applying for. Highlight your strong qualities and key professional skills that you have formed during all the years of work. Of course, you need to identify those that the employer indicated in the job description. *You* are not your job. Hence, your interviewer doesn't need to know your favorite food or the number siblings you have. Highlight personal interests that are relevant to this situation and position.

In order to disclose the job seeker, the recruiter does not need to invent anything. It is enough to ask a person to tell about himself. A recruiter understands that what and how a person tells about himself speaks for itself. Often, the interviewer uses special pauses. He does not say anything but continues to look at the candidate in a friendly manner. What does he expect in return? Ideally, you should pause or independently ask the question, 'Do I need to clarify the information?' Describe your strengths and weaknesses. It's not a great idea to list your flaws and negative personality traits in an attempt to appear modest and honest. Instead of *listing* them, portray the traits that you perceive to be weaknesses as qualities that you are working on, endeavoring to turn them into strengths. It is best to talk about those traits that have nothing to do with

a particular job. You can recollect the features that you worked on and were corrected. For example, what you achieved after completing training, mastering the techniques of time management, etc. The main thing is to show that your weaknesses will not affect future work in any way.

At the risk of sounding overbearing or boastful, don't list your strengths either. Rather speak of an instance where one or two of your strengths helped in a work-related situation. Read the list of requirements for vacancies in advance and select 3-4 qualities that are best compared with the requirements of the employer. For example, if you are employed as an interpreter, talk about your linguistic qualities, and if this is a PR manager's position, talk about creative and non-standard approaches to work.

If you are a highly organized individual who is pedantic about neatness and order, these personality traits can be highlighted if you are applying for a position as a legal secretary. But they may be less needed if you are

applying for a post as a nursery school teacher.

Question type 2: How would your friends you?

Interviewers use this question to determine if your personality will fit the role for which you are interviewed and the culture of the company to which you are applying. Describe yourself as your friends would; bear in mind the traits and characteristics that fit this situation. You can say 'My friends tell me that I am friendly and that I'm a real people-person.' One of them jokes that I could sell ice to an Inuit (smiling)." This type of answer would be great if you are applying for a sales position.

Question type 3: Would you consider yourself to be innovative?

This is not a 'yes/no' question. This is an *entry point* on which to elaborate. With the advancement of technology and the constant change in trends, employers are looking for people who are inventive and pioneering; people who can break ground in new areas and take the company to new places. You will use this opportunity to tell of a time when you had an idea that was relevant and was implemented successfully.

For example, environmental sustainability is of great concern, and businesses are all climbing on board; environmental awareness promotes good business amongst like-minded customers. You could tell of the time that you suggested to your accounts department that they email all bills and statements to clients instead of using the postal service. This exercise not only saved some trees but also saved the company a fair amount of money on postage.

Question type 4: How do you deal with conflict in the office?

This question is asked so that the interviewer can understand if you are or not a team player. Your best answer to this question would be to give a real life example of a conflict situation that had a positive outcome. Unfortunately, different personality types do clash, and where there are different ideas, there will be differences of opinion. The focus here will be to prove that you were able to resolve issues amicably without resorting to anger, manipulation, or bribery and corruption to get your way. It is important to note that a peace-maker is not the same as someone who shies away from conflict. You may have escaped conflict in the office because you chose to avoid it rather than resolve it.

Question type 5: How do you ensure that your skills are current?

Staying up-to-date and being eager to learn and grow in your field of occupation proves that you enjoy your job and have an interest in your career. This is where you would mention courses you have taken, seminars you have attended, mentorship programs you have participated in, or autobiographies that you have read. At this stage, you can enquire about the company's staff training programs to support your willingness to learn and grow.

Question type 6: Can you describe your perfect job?

Here the interviewer is trying to ascertain whether or not you are a good fit for the company. This may tempt you into waffling about corner offices, personal assistants, and a six-digit salary – but does *that* describe *this* job? Focus on your skills and strengths, weave in your core responsibilities, and describe them in light of the requirements for this job.

Question type 7: What don't or didn't you like about your current or previous job?

Asking this question, the employer wants to better know your background and understand the reasons and criteria for finding a new job. Do not be lured into venting all your existing work frustrations. You can make a bad impression. If you break into a rant about a selfish boss, arduous tasks, and irritating colleagues, you are going to make your interviewer wonder if *you* are not actually the problematic common factor. Somehow, compliment the company but reiterate your need for personal expansion and growth – hence your desire to move on to the greater opportunity that this new position offers you. At the same time, you must not forget that the answer should be based on your professional plans.

Question type 8: What salary would you like to earn?

When looking for work, one must be guided by one's needs and clearly, remember the expenditure part of the family budget. But making one's expenses by justifying the level of wages is not the most beneficial policy.

Research the average rates for the job so that you don't aim too high or too low. This information is easily accessible on various salary guide websites. Your interview is not the place to negotiate your rate; negotiation starts only once an offer of employment has been made. An important point is you need not just to name the figure in the interview, but you also need to be ready to justify the amount to the employer. Explain to the employer why your professional skills are worth exactly that much in accordance with how unique and necessary the company-employer skills you possess.

Also don't forget the basis for getting financial reward should be, first of all, your professional skills. After all, companies don't buy your financial expectations, experience, and skills. The employer has his own business process for which he is ready to spend certain funds. It's nothing personal, it's just business.

Question type 9: Where do you see yourself in five years?

Any employer wants to hire a motivated and interested employee. Therefore, when asking this question, he wants to understand how much your career plans are comparable to the proposed vacancy. Accordingly, the employer wants to know how passionate you will feel about the work, how long you plan to work for the company, etc. When answering this question, try to demonstrate as much enthusiasm as possible, if possible, show the connection between your professional plans and this post.

Question type 10: Why do you consider this vacancy as an important element of the career path?

Avoid the clichéd answer of, 'In your seat.' This was funny in the 90's. Be honest about realistic future goals. In terms of an occupation, five years is a relatively short period. Explain how *this* position fits into your career plans. Reiterate that your greatest priority is to dedicate your time and energy to this new opportunity and that you hope to earn promotions through hard work and dedication.

Do not admit that you want to climb the corporate ladder even if it means using different jobs in your attempt to get there. Do not say that by that time you want to own your own company or travel around the world. No company wants to invest time and funds training and honing an individual if they understand that they have plans to flit off somewhere else within a short period of time.

Dealing with Inappropriate Questions

Although it is unnecessary and inappropriate (in some instances illegal) to ask questions regarding race, gender, age, religion, marital status, sexual orientation and political views, these questions do sometimes slip through the cracks. The best way to answer without causing conflict would be to state that you see no relevance between the

question and the position you are applying for.

Examples of Behavior-Based Interview Questions

Question 1: Can you give an example of how you work under pressure?

You can tell of a time when you and your team had a very important deadline looming. You arranged that each team member committed an extra hour of their day to the completion of the task. Thanks to your hard-working team and your efficient management, the project was completed in time.

Question 2: Was there a time when you failed?

Don't be tempted to say, 'I have never failed.' Everyone makes mistakes. Your prospective employer is not trying to trip you up or humiliate you by asking about your past failures. He is simply trying to ascertain how you deal with situations that don't go according to plan. Tell of missed deadlines or lost reports, and then make sure you mention the lessons you learned from the slip-ups and how you will apply these lessons in future.

Question 3: Can you give an example of a goal you reached and explain how you attained it?

Everyone has a dream – but a goal is a dream that comes with an action plan. If you wanted to be floor manager from the first day you step into a department store as a cashier, be sure to mention how you took night classes and worked longer shifts so that you could receive on-the-job training. Talk about your goal in a positive way and attribute your success to perseverance.

Question 4: Have you ever implemented a decision that was not popular?

There are times when leaders have to do things that others may not like or appreciate. If there was a time that you had to cut back on lunch hours to complete a project or swap people's shifts to ensure greater efficiency, you will share these examples as well as the methods you used to placate your staff so that they were not too disgruntled.

Question 5: How did you deal with an irate customer?

Without bad-mouthing the person, you can relay an experience where a customer or client became angry because of a mistake you made or due to any other misunderstanding. Be sure to end on a positive note and state how the situation was resolved amicably. If you were not senior personnel, mention if you called on senior staff to help you resolve issues that were above your capacity to solve and state the lesson learned from the experience.

Chapter 5 - Statements to Avoid During an Interview

The success of your interview doesn't only depend on how you say, but what you say. You should not say things that can provoke an undesired reaction from the interviewer. You need to avoid forbidden statements/phrases – that would be of help to you. Consider the following:

1. *'I don't know.'*

Regardless of which interviewer's question, you are answering, never say this. In any case, it will produce a negative impression on the employer. Such an answer from the applicant tells the employer that such applicant did not prepare for the interview. Moreover, he does not even try to correct the situation; it reflects something been invented on the move or the applicant is trying to get out somehow in order not to disappoint the employer.

2. *'Everything is written on my resume, what exactly do I tell you?'*

You could say this statement in response to the interviewer's request to tell about yourself. If it's hard for you to retell or expand on what you wrote on the resume, then you don't need the work you are applying for. Maybe you just do not know how to present yourself. It's not thinking aloud. Such conclusion can make the interviewer uncomfortable. Do not create such an image of yourself in the interviewer's eyes. Repeat information about yourself from your resume. Give specific examples to confirm what you wrote.

3. 'Never,' 'never,' 'no one,' 'for nothing,' 'not ...'

You can't often say negations when you talk about past jobs. (Examples: "didn't appreciate," 'no one did anything,' etc.) This will cause an alarm for your potential employer. Any expressive and categorical expressions show that the job seeker is difficult to restrain his emotions. Most likely, this is a symptom of the fact that the job seeker had professional problems in the past. For example, conflicts with colleagues or a leader.

4. "I am ready to do everything!"

Many job seekers mistakenly believe that such dedication will only please the employer. But this is not so. If an interviewee says such, it means he does not yet understand in which direction he would like to develop, and the knowledge and skills he will deepen in. In addition, the willingness to do everything can give an insecure person (someone who feels that he can 'sell' himself to the employer). Using such tactics, the job seeker tries to persuade the employer to hire him.

5. 'What will be my responsibilities?'

This question shows you an overly confident candidate for a job. The competitor should not speak at interview as if he had already been invited to work (examples: 'How many people will I have in my subordination?' 'What will be required of me?') Such make the employer reject the job seeker. Remember this!

If you don't want to make a negative impression, it's best to ask questions from the position of the third person about the company's activities. For example: 'What results do you expect from a person who will take this position?'

6. *'I haven't questioned.'*

As a rule, at the end of the interview, the interviewer asks, 'Do you have any questions?' If the candidate has no questions, most likely, the result of the interview will be negative. Still ask questions, even if you understand everything. Questions can relate to the scope of your potential work, goals, organizational structure and the corporate culture of the company. On the eve of the interview, you are advised to prepare a short list of questions. Otherwise, the interviewer will think that the job seeker is not interested in working in their company.

It's hard not to agree that if a person has a huge desire to receive an invitation to a particular company, then he should have additional questions. Since the job seeker wants to know more information about the company. If the job seeker does not ask anything, this raises doubts with the employer.

7. *'Do you have other vacancies?'*

Usually, this is spoken by young professionals who are struggling to find work; although they could be forgiven, but not so for specialists with experience. Why? At first, this question says it is important for a person not to get into a particular company, but simply to find a job somewhere. Secondly, it shows the uncertainty of the candidate. Not knowing the verdict of the employer, the candidate immediately recognizes that he did not pass the interview.

Chapter 6 - Finishing Strong

A racecar driver does not slow down as he approaches the finish line; instead, he accelerates to ensure a strong finish. Your interview should reflect this analogy. Don't fizzle out at the end and leave the room timidly. Here are some ideas to help you and your interview on a winning streak.

Prepare Some of Your Own Questions for the Interview

Very often interviewers will give you a chance to ask them some questions. Asking a few well-prepared questions proves a genuine interest in the position. Pay attention during the interview, as some of your questions may well be answered. If by this stage of the interview all of your questions *have* been answered, be sure to mention this so that the interviewer knows you are not simply copping out. You could jot down key words to remind yourself of questions or queries that may spring to mind during the interview.

Questions You May Want to Ask During an Interview

Sample Question 1: What is the first thing you would expect from the successful candidate?

This question will give you an indication of what is in store for you when you start the job. If you have applied for a position in marketing and the answer to the question is, 'We expect you to cold-call prospects and reach a target of one hundred customers within your first month, thereafter you will service and maintain these customers.'

If cold-calling gives you sleepless nights, then you may want to reconsider the position.

Ask a specific question about the company based on your relevant research. This will affirm your interest in the company and prove that you took the time to do some investigation before your interview. For example: 'I read on www.financebizz.com that your company is planning an expansion into Africa. How long do you think this will take to implement and will you be sending staff from here to train staff there?'

Sample Question 2: 'What do you like most about working for this company?'

The company, like you, is also trying to showcase their best side. By asking an existing employee what they like most, you will get an idea of the real benefits that the company offers. The answers you receive will be relative to the person you ask. Some people will enjoy the convenience of the cafeteria or lunchroom; others will enjoy getting a day off on their birthday, whereas another set of employees may appreciate the medical or pension plan. Whichever it is, you should be able to tell a lot about how a company takes care of their staff by asking this question.

Sample Question 3: 'Would you mind showing me around and introducing me to some of the people I may work with?'

This indicates that you are very keen on the job and interested in the company. It also gives you the opportunity to view the working environment, working conditions and colleague interaction.

Sample Question 4: 'Can you think of an obvious reason why I am not a good fit for this position?'

Asking this question may give you time to clarify any misunderstandings that may have taken place during the interview. Possibly when you mentioned that you love traveling, the interviewer may have assumed that you would constantly be asking for leave.

The Final Lap

When your interview draws to an end, thank the interviewer for his time; confirm that you enjoyed the interview, reiterate that you are still keen on the position and that you feel you are the right person for the job. Ask when you can expect to hear from them regarding the outcome of the interview. End off as resolutely as you began.

The day after your interview, send an email or write a letter and deliver it to the person who interviewed you. Maybe you have thought of a question in the interim. Maybe a statement made during the interview sparked an idea you want to share. Definitely thank them again for the opportunity. The *content* of the letter is not as important as the *purpose* of the letter – it serves to remind them that you are interested, that you are communicative, that you are innovative, and that you are functional. It will make them *remember* who you are and possibly aid in making you stand out from the rest of the applicants.

If Worse Comes to Worst

If for some reason you really mess up during the interview, don't give up. If you feel that this job would be a good fit for you, contact the interviewer with a phone call or via email and express the fact that you were not on top

form. Ask for the opportunity to try again and reiterate what you believe you have to offer the company which may have been overshadowed by extreme nervousness during the meeting. This approach may help – but if you don't give it a shot, you will never know. We can't win them all; some jobs are going to slip through your fingers. Don't lose heart; treat each interview as a learning curve. If you can take the experience and learn something from it, then you are still a winner!

Made in the USA
Columbia, SC
18 August 2017